KITTEN PACK

THE
OWNER'S
HANDBOOK

CLAIRE ARROWSMITH

B.Sc. (Hons), M.Sc.

BOWTIE
P R E S S®
www.bowtiepress.com

First published in the USA and Canada
by BowTie Press
A Division of BowTie, Inc.
3 Burroughs
Irvine, CA 92618
www.bowtiepress.com

Library of Congress
Cataloging-in-Publication Data

Arrowsmith, Claire.
  The kitten pack : making the most of
kitty's first year / by Claire
Arrowsmith.
     p. cm.
  Includes index.
  ISBN 978-1-933958-69-9
  1. Kittens--Handbooks, manuals, etc. I.
Title.

SF447.A77 2009
636.8--dc22

2009004060

The Author

Claire Arrowsmith was raised in the Highlands of Scotland with a range of domestic, farm, and wild animals that fueled her love of and interest in all animals, particularly cats and dogs. Claire is a full member of the Association of Pet Behaviour Counsellors (APBC) and runs her own behavioral consultancy. She holds an Honours degree in Zoology and a Masters degree in Applied Animal Behaviour and Animal Welfare. Claire has worked in animal rescue and with Hearing Dogs for Deaf People. She is also the specialist behaviorist for Houndstar Films, which produces cat, dog, and small animal advisory DVDs.

She is the author of *What If My Cat?* (with Francesca Riccomini) and *The Sit, Down, Come, Heel, Stay and Stand Book.* She currently lives in England with her husband, Ross, their kitten, Pickle, and their Rhodesian Ridgeback mix, Sarnie.

Printed in China
through Printworks Int Ltd
13 12 11 10 09   1 2 3 4 5

Acknowledgments

I would like to thank the cat breeders who offered such good advice to me during the course of writing this book, and also say thank you to Ruth for reading through the text and for making great suggestions. Your help was greatly appreciated.

The recommendations in this book are given without any guarantees on the part of the author and publisher. If in doubt, seek the advice of a vet or pet-care specialist.

CONTENTS

CHOOSING YOUR KITTEN

Cats have become the most commonly owned household pet in recent years and for most of us, it's easy to see why. Friendly cats provide their owners with welcome companionship and allow many people to experience the joys of pet ownership.

Seniors benefit from the social interaction, comfort and routine that a cat provides. Children can learn about the responsibilities of pet ownership from their parents while spending time caring for and entertaining their feline friend. Every cat owner would probably give a different reason why they chose their cat or why their pet is so special to them.

Expert Tip
Good kitten care must include financial provisions for vet fees, quality food, toys, litter, bedding, scratching posts, and possibly, pet insurance.

Why Do You Want a Kitten?
- Companionship
- As a pet for your children
- As a companion for another cat
- Ideal choice for apartment or condo living
- A pet that doesn't require being taken outside to exercise
- To show or breed

below: **The kitten-owner bond can be very strong.**

Understanding exactly what your expectations of cat ownership are will help you choose one that's most suited to you. You will have to be prepared for the responsibility that owning a cat brings. It is a myth that a cat isn't sociable and that he won't need much attention. Although a cat may seem like an easier pet than a dog because he doesn't need walking, he still relies on you for his care. Cats require daily attention, social interaction, and lots of patience, especially when they're young. A kitten is bursting with energy, and his mischievous nature will need to be prepared for and understood. Taking on a kitten will mean that you will have to be responsible for his care throughout his life, which is typically 15 to 18 years. It's vital to look after your kitten properly because if his feline needs are not being met, then he will become unhappy and frustrated, and you could face behavioral or health problems. You are responsible for your kitten's well-being throughout his life and should be prepared for this—so plan ahead. Every day cats are relinquished to animal shelters or even euthanized because they are unwanted or have

below: **Your kitten will require plenty of activity and playtime.**

right: **A young kitten will love being with you each day.**

right: **Spend time with your kitten to prevent boredom.**

behavioral problems that the owner cannot cope with. For these reasons, thinking carefully about what kind of life you can offer a cat is very important.

What Kind of Kitten?

The vast majority of pet cats are actually randomly bred, and since they come in such a wonderful array of colors and temperaments, there's usually one to suit all types of owners. These are also referred to as mixed breeds, or domestic short- or longhair cats. However, for cat lovers looking for something more specific, there are more than 70 recognized breeds and dozens of color and marking variations available. This variety can initially be confusing for people unfamiliar with cats.

Pedigree Cats

Cat breeds are divided up into categories that differ slightly depending on the country and organization. Some, such as the CFA (The Cat Fanciers' Association) and GCCF (Governing Council of the Cat Fancy), register the more traditional breeds, while other groups such as TICA (The International Cat Association) allow newer breeds and more color variations to be recognized. All major organizations will regularly run cat shows and provide as much information as possible for prospective owners.

> **Expert Tip**
> A kitten does a lot of growing. During the first 5 months, a kitten increases in size about 2,000 percent from his birth weight. Kittens also need about twice as many calories per pound of body weight as adult cats do, so pay attention to their feeding regimens.

Which Breed?

One of the best ways to learn about cat breeds is to view them at a show and talk to their owners. Cat organizations advertise their events on their Web sites and through cat magazines.

Once you've determined what kind of cat you like, there will be lots of information available about breed types and their history and temperament. Cat characters vary as much as their looks, so it's important to do your research carefully. Remember to research lots of sources so you can get a complete, unbiased picture of the lifestyle each breed is most suited to and the type of character it is likely to have.

A Good Breeder

When choosing your breeder, you must also research the pedigree line your kitten will come from. Breeders will vary in their experience and in the quality of the kittens they produce. Because some pedigrees have small gene pools, there has been a high level of interbreeding, which has

above: **The Scottish Fold displays distinctive ears.**

resulted in some kittens carrying or suffering from inherited diseases or behavioral problems. These problems can affect the cat's quality of life and prevent you from showing or breeding. Good breeders will make the health and welfare of their cats and kittens of prime importance. You may have to travel to find the perfect kitten, but taking time to choose the right one is worth every moment.

right: **Maine Coon cats can grow quite large. They are generally good-tempered.**

The Differences Among Breed Groups

Mixed Breed (often referred to as Domestic Shorthair [DSH] or Domestic Longhair [DLH], or random bred)	Might come in any combination of color or coat length. Although the size range in cats is not vast, this will depend on the parentage.	Temperament will vary depending upon the cat's genetics and history.
Cross-breed	Occurs when two different pedigrees are bred together.	Will show some of the characteristics of both parental breeds.
Persians or Himalayans	Ancient breeds with a long, thick coat that needs daily grooming. These breeds are usually relaxed and sociable but not athletic.	Usually have more laid-back personalities and are typically inactive.
Other Longhaired Pedigree Cats	Includes various sizes and coat types, such as Ragdoll, Maine Coon, and Norwegian Forest Cat.	Vary from extremely laid-back characters to very independent, athletic cats.
British Shorthairs	A sturdy, round-faced attractive cat.	Can be independent but will enjoy your attention.
American Shorthairs	Strong, muscular cats derived from early domestic cats and larger than British versions.	Typically relaxed, robust characters.
Oriental Cats	This group includes a wide range of energetic breeds like the Bengal and Ocicat. Sizes will vary between breeds.	Usually have a lively, extrovert, character. They require company and lots of stimulation so are not suited to a solitary life if you work full-time.

Your Preferences and Lifestyle

Choosing the right kitten for you will involve thinking about what you want from your pet and what you can offer it in return. Be honest with yourself about how much time, money, and effort you can devote to your kitten. The following table may help you to match up your preferences with the available cat types:

Pedigree Cat

- You can research and prepare for the type of cat that you are buying.
- You know what size, coat type, and possibly temperament to expect.
- May need more health care.
- Breeder often more experienced.
- Genetic history available.
- More expensive to purchase.

Mixed Breed

- Characteristics will be a surprise.
- The kitten may grow larger or smaller than expected.
- Coats will vary in length and look.
- Fewer inherited health issues.
- Often from a shelter or the streets.
- Unknown genetic history.
- May be free or quite inexpensive.

Male Cat

- May be more territorial.
- May be more likely to spray mark.
- Likely to be larger than female.
- Will roam to find a mate if not castrated.
- If unneutered, will have stronger scent.
- More likely to fight.
- Cheaper to neuter than a female.

Female Cat

- May attract males if she comes into season.
- "Calling" will occur if left intact.
- Smaller than males.
- Can be more sensitive in nature.
- Unplanned litters may occur if intact and has access to males.
- Costs more to spay than a male.

Longhair Cat

- Will require daily grooming to prevent mats developing in coat.
- Needs to tolerate handling.
- Possibly extra expense of professional groomer.
- Will influence the type of cat litter you can use.

Shorthair Cat

- Weekly groom only to keep coat healthy and clean.
- Grooming takes less time.
- Normally keeps itself very clean.
- Unlikely to need a professional groomer.
- Clumping litter less likely to stick to hair and paws.

Questions to Consider

- Will you offer safe access to the outdoors through use of enclosures and harnesses?
- If not, do you have adequate space for an indoor-only cat
- Will the kitten live with children?
- Are your current pets cat friendly?
- Will you tolerate a noisy cat?
- Would you prefer an active cat or a lazy lap cat?
- Will you have the time and patience for the daily grooming of a long coat?
- How do you feel about cat hair being shed in your house?
- Do any of your family members suffer from allergies to cat hair?

Choosing an Older or Rescue Cat

After considering your options, you may decide that an older cat is a good choice, as you'll have some knowledge of his personality. There are many cat rescue groups with full facilities waiting for sympathetic prospective owners. Choose a reputable group so that you know that the cats have been well cared for and have been health-checked by a veterinarian. Living in a shelter can be stressful for many cats, so take your time and don't immediately dismiss a quieter cat. Asking questions and spending time with the cat will help you choose wisely.

If you want a pedigree adult cat, then try contacting the breed rescue or appropriate breeders. Breeders often have older cats who are not suitable for showing or breeding but who make perfect pets.

Choosing Two Kittens

If you work and believe that you could financially cope with more than one kitten, then adopting two siblings may be ideal. They'll provide company and fun for each other. However, you must remember to spend lots of time with both kittens so that they continue to grow in

> **Expert Tips**
> - Be honest with yourself about your lifestyle before you pick a kitten.
> - Ask for breeder recommendations from your veterinarian.
> - Buy a kitten only if you're confident of his health and breeding.

confidence and learn to love human contact, too. Owning two or more cats does require you to provide more resources such as bowls, litter boxes, beds, and toys. You should budget to cover the cost of insurance as well as surgical costs to have them neutered at the appropriate age.

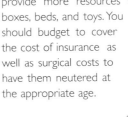

Not all cats can cope around children.

above: **Games can help build bonds.**

below: **Kittens can enjoy the company of others.**

Finding the Perfect Kitten

Once you have decided on the type of kitten you want, you'll need to spend time finding the ideal source. If you prefer a non-pedigree cat, then call local animal shelters, rescue groups, and veterinary clinics for information about litters in your area.

You may have to time your adoption for kittens at animal shelters. Spring tends to be "kitten season." For pedigree kittens, contact the breed clubs for information about current litters and for a list of registered breeders.

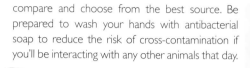

Choosing a Breeder

When you first call breeders, you should try to get as much information as possible so you can decide whether or not they're right for you. Find out what the breeders do with their cats (are they mainly pets or purely for show?) and where the cats live (indoors or in a cat enclosure?). Ask how many litters are bred each year and how many litters this particular queen has had (ideally no more than one each year). Ask what they do to socialize their kittens to prepare them for life's events. If you like what you hear, then make an appointment to view the kittens.

It's often a good idea to visit more than one litter of kittens so that you can compare and choose from the best source. Be prepared to wash your hands with antibacterial soap to reduce the risk of cross-contamination if you'll be interacting with any other animals that day.

What to Look For

- Lively, happy kittens with healthy, clean coats, eyes, and ears. Diarrhea, weepy eyes, or runny noses can be signs of serious health problems.
- The kittens shouldn't seem too thin, nor should they have pot bellies, which could indicate worms.
- The kittens should take an interest in their surroundings and seem playful.
- You should be able to meet the mother (the queen), and she should be able to access her kittens freely.
- Kittens over three weeks should have a litter box available.
- The area where the kittens live should be clean and fresh.
- Pedigree paperwork and veterinary records should be available for your inspection.

With the breeder's permission, carefully pick up each kitten and gently stroke it while talking in a calm, quiet voice. If you have any misgivings about how quiet the kittens are, then you could visit again at another time when they're not sleepy from eating or playing. Additionally, as the weeks pass, the personalities of each kitten will become clearer, so it's worth visiting the litters more than once, giving you a chance to observe the kittens' respective

left: Observe the kittens with their mother to get a feel for their characters and health.

tempered father has been shown to be important in influencing the character of his offspring.

Making the choice—Be sensible and choose a healthy, sociable kitten. Picking an ill kitten because you feel sorry for him is a bad idea, as he could encourage further poor breeding and care. Try to choose the kitten that matches your requirements closely. Some breeders and many animal shelters may want to do a home check, in which they visit you to ensure that everything is safe and suitable for one of their kittens before you get to take him home.

Deposit—This is often required for a breeder to keep a specific kitten for you. Be aware that this money is often nonrefundable if you change your mind.

Check for clean, bright eyes, nose, and ears.

above: **Breeders often encourage you to visit to see the cats and to discuss your needs.**

Gently examine the kittens to check for signs of ill health.

characters. The breeder should be happy to discuss with you his or her methods for socializing and handling the young kittens.

The parents—The mother should be healthy and friendly (though it's natural for her to be a little cautious while you're handling her kittens). You may also be able to meet the sire. A well-

KITTEN PAPERWORK

If you're buying a pedigree kitten, then you should expect to receive a receipt, a contract of sale, pedigree papers, and registration documents. The pedigree is a record of the kitten's family tree, while the registration confirms that it has been formally acknowledged by a feline governing body and is recognized as a pedigree of that breed. If the cat is already registered to the breeder, you should both sign a transfer form (or ownership papers) before you take your kitten home.

Some kittens will also come with endorsement papers that will state any

above: **In all the excitement, don't forget to collect your receipt and important documents.**

stipulations you have agreed to. For example, the breeder may believe that your kitten carries a trait that makes him less than ideal for breeding. If you do breed, the resulting kittens will not be able to be registered. These should be available at the time of purchase. If you are buying a mixed breed

cat, then there will be less paperwork. A receipt, health records, and occasionally conditions of sale will be available but pedigree or registration documents won't exist. Always remember that papers don't guarantee a good, healthy kitten, so make sure you assess the breeder and the litter and ask lots of questions before you buy.

Receipt—This will state the amount of money you have paid the breeder or the animal shelter for your kitten. You should receive a receipt for any deposit you have paid and for the remaining balance when you collect your kitten. If you insure your cat against theft or death, then this receipt will be used to prove the monetary value of your cat. Any extras you have bought from the breeder (such as litter, food, and so on), should be itemized separately on the receipt.

A contract of sale—This is a legal document stating the names of the seller and buyer of the kitten. This contract will vary between breeders' so make sure you read it thoroughly and understand the agreement before you pay for your kitten. Animal shelters will have their own standard sales contract and will normally ask you to agree not to breed your kitten and to have him neutered at the appropriate time.

Pedigree papers—You'll receive a completed pedigree documentation signed by the breeder showing at least three generations.

Important Details

When you purchase your kitten, there are some important details that you should know. In all cases other than some rescue cases, you should be told the kitten's date of birth.

Pedigree kittens will have a registered name, and you should note the breeder's name and affix (see pages 14–15), which should be registered, with a cat governing body. Additional information regarding any veterinary health checks and treatments the kitten has had should also be included in the information pack you receive.

Your breeder may add clauses regarding permissions for breeding if you have that planned for your kitten. Breeders often include a clause ensuring that the cat is returned to them for rehoming if the new owner's situation changes or if there are unforeseen problems requiring that the cat be returned.

Occasionally a breeder will add other miscellaneous clauses into the contract. These may involve agreements about exporting, breeding, or showing your kitten. Read your full contract carefully, as it is a legally binding document. A written contract also normally includes a health guarantee. Take your new kitten to your veterinary clinic within the first two weeks to ensure that he is developing normally.

Signing the Contract

As for most legal documents, you will be required to sign and date the contract at the end. The breeder will also sign alongside your name. You will both be required to state your addresses. There should be two copies of the contract; one for you to keep and one for the breeder's records. Both parties should have copies of all relevant endorsements and health records.

Checklist of Important Paperwork

- Receipt
- Contract of sale
- Pedigree papers
- Registration documents
- Health records

It's important that your new kitten is examined by your vet. Besides spotting early signs of problems, your vet will also advise on necessary vaccinations and parasite prevention.

What's in a Pedigree?

A pedigree cat will have a known family line that extends back over several generations. The breeder will be able to provide you with the kitten's family tree going back perhaps five generations. Each relative will be from the same registered breed.

The pedigree paperwork will also state information about the cat, such as championship titles or such genetic traits as eye or coat color. You will receive a printed or handwritten pedigree. You can also obtain a copy from the governing body where your cat is registered.

Kittens who have not been registered cannot be assumed to be pure pedigree and will not be eligible for breeding or showing as pure breeds. A pedigree kitten registered as Non-Active should never be bred. If you intend to show your kitten competitvely, then check the pedigree against the registration regulations to make sure that she qualifies. Breeders will often advise on which of their kittens have potential as show quality cats and which have disqualifying marks or features. No guarantee can be made, however, as to how suitable a kitten may be for showing when mature.

Common Abbreviations You May Find in Your Kitten's Pedigree

CH: Champion (CFA). This is the first level and indicates that the cat has won six winner's ribbons at shows. Other organizations have different requirements.

PR: Premier (CFA). Neutered cats have their own groups, and Premier is their equivalent to the Champion level.

GC: Grand Champion (TICA). This cat has achieved over 200 points in competitions. Requirements vary between organizations and it may be listed as GRC, GCH, or Gr Ch.

GCA: Grand Champion Alter. This is the category for neutered cats achieving sufficient credits through competition.

IC: International Champion (FIFe) level comes after the cat has achieved Champion level (FIFe).

RW: Regional Winner (CFA).

NW: National Winner (CFA).

EC: European Champion (CFA).

QGC: Quadruple Grand Champion (ACFA, TICA).

DM: Distinguished Merit is awarded to cats that have produced winning offspring. Females must have produced five grand champions, and males 15 grand champions.

WW: World Winner (FIFe). This prestigious title is awarded to cats who have achieved best of category at the World Show.

These abbreviations are earned through winning competitions at cat shows. Breeders have to work hard to get their cats to the top standard, and they dedicate a lot of time and money getting to shows and in caring for their cats appropriately. If you don't know what any of the abbreviations mean in your kitten's pedigree, then ask the breeder. Many abbreviations exist and they can seem confusing until they are explained. Some additional letters simply indicate traits like coat type or eye color (BEW = Blue-eyed white, CPC= Color-point carrier) so that breeders can assess the gene transfer more accurately.

Affix or Kennel Names

Breeders may also include their own affix at the start of their kittens' pedigree names. This easily identifies a cat's origin and line of ancestry. You might spot a cat with the kennel name positioned at the end of the registered name. This is called a suffix and identifies cats that have been bred elsewhere but are now owned by this breeder.

The pedigree abbreviation list is so extensive as there are many awards and levels that cats may achieve that are granted by the different cat organizations. The organizations you are likely to encounter include:

ACFA: American Cat Fanciers Association

FIFe: Fédération Internationale Féline

GCCF: Governing Council of the Cat Fancy

CCA: Canadian Cat Association

CFA: The Cat Fanciers' Association

TICA: The International Cat Association

left: **Winning shows takes a lot of time and dedication. If you're interested in showing, make sure your kitten has show potential by talking to the breeder and picking carefully. The cat organizations will provide information about registration and show dates.**

right: **Within a pedigree litter, there will be variation in color and size and shape. Your breeder will advise you on the kitten best suited for you.**

EQUIPMENT YOU WILL NEED

Litter Box
Choose a litter box that your kitten can easily get into (high sides might cause a problem until he grows bigger). It can help to choose one similar in style to the one used by the breeder so that your kitten doesn't become confused.

Litter
Be prepared to buy a good-quality litter. It should absorb urine well and be easy to rake over. Nontoxic products are important, as kittens often eat small amounts of litter while playing and investigating this material. Start with the litter type used by the breeder or shelter.

above: **It is sensible to invest in a good-quality litter box and cleaning scoop.**

Food
Your breeder or vet can advise you on the proper food for your newly adopted kitten. There are special kitten diets suited for your kitten's tiny mouth and teeth. Remember that very young kittens can struggle with dry kibble.

Food and Water Bowls
Stainless steel and ceramic bowls are easy to clean and should be heavy enough to prevent them tipping over if the kitten paws on them. Plastic bowls are cheaper but can harbor parasites if the surfaces become nicked, which can lead to a skin condition called contact dermatitis. Have separate bowls to ensure that fresh water is always available. Cats tend not to drink much, so a drinking fountain can encourage your kitten to take in the water necessary for good health.

Beds
Cats love warm, secure places and may not appreciate expensive cat beds. However, beds in carefully positioned baskets or cushioned window perches are usually well liked.

Bedding
This can be made from sheets or blankets that you already own or can be bought specifically for your kitten. They should be washable. Take care to remove loose threads that could be chewed and swallowed. Some breeds, especially the Siamese, can become compulsive about sucking and chewing woollen articles, so monitor any damage and remove the offending items.

Cat Carrier
This is an essential piece of equipment, as your kitten needs to be transported safely to and from the veterinary clinic and during

above: **A nonslip bowl allows your kitten to eat and drink comfortably without spilling.**

above: **Fleece beds can easily be washed or vacuumed and they particularly suit cats who love to be cozy.**

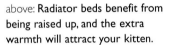

above: **Radiator beds benefit from being raised up, and the extra warmth will attract your kitten.**

right: **A sturdy cat carrier is a necessity. It is also useful for making safe introductions to other pets.**

car trips. A carrier will ensure that your kitten doesn't escape while you travel. A carrier that can be opened up at the top as well as at the front will allow your kitten to be removed without being tipped or pulled out. Your kitten will become familiar with the carrier, and this will make it easier each time you need to make a visit to the vet. If you intend to make longer journeys with your cat, then choose a larger carrier with built-in food and water bowls.

Safety Tip

When choosing a toy, avoid any material that could be ingested, and keep toys with long strings or pointed parts for use during supervised play only.

Toys

Kittens are very active, so it is important to provide a range of playthings. Paper wads, feather wands, Ping-Pong balls, and soft toy mice are good picks. Your kitten's favorite toy may vary, depending upon his mood, energy level, age, and whether he is playing with you, with another cat, or alone.

right: **Cat toys come in a variety of shapes, colors, and types to suit all your kitten's characteristics and moods. Damaged toys should be replaced to avoid any risk of injury.**

Other Useful Items

Scratching post—Posts are available in many sizes and designs. An upright post allows your kitten to scratch by reaching up and scratching downward (an alternative to taking it out on the wallpaper or curtains). A horizontal surface allows him to reach forward and scratch back toward himself (an alternative

right: **A scratching post will help prevent destructive behavior problems.**

to using carpets, furniture, or rugs). Each cat has his own preferences about where and how he likes to scratch, and this will dictate the type of scratching post you should provide. Kittens benefit from having both options available. Posts are commonly made from sisal string or carpet fabric. Brand-new posts may not be as attractive to some cats, so tease out some of the threads and—after your kitten is 6 months old—sprinkle organic catnip to spark his interest.

Grooming brush and comb—All cats require grooming to keep their coats in ideal condition. Longer coats require more intensive care. You will need a variety of brushes and combs to suit your cat's coat. Your grooming kit should include various combs, brushes, a flea comb, wipes, nail clippers, and styptic powder.

Collar and tag—Collars must be suitable for cats with an elasticated section or a breakaway buckle to allow easy escape if your cat should become caught on a branch or fence outside. The tag should have your name and telephone number on it. Collars can be lost— and indoor cats escape—so ask your vet about having your kitten microchipped.

Cat door—Once he's old enough to venture into the outside world under your supervision, a cat door is an easy way to allow your kitten safe access to an outdoor enclosure. Sadly, there are far too many dangers facing unchaperoned kittens, ranging from coyotes to cars, to allow cats to roam. Cat doors or flaps come in many varieties and can be fitted through doors, windows or walls. You can choose from simple flaps the cat just pushes through to ones that open when triggered by a magnet on your cat's collar or, most recently, by your cat's microchip. There are cat flaps for all budgets as well as types of outdoor enclosures. Your kitten may take time to learn to use a heavy flap or may be startled by one that shuts noisily behind him, so choose a quality product. Most cat flaps can be locked by the owner, which is useful if you find that neighborhood cats are entering your property during the night. Consider adding a cat tree or perch in the outdoor enclosure to allow your cat to enjoy the outdoors from a high perch.

Get your kitten used to being brushed.

First Aid Kit

All cat owners should gather together a basic first aid kit in case of emergency. It should contain the items recommended below. It is also sensible to keep a note of your vet's telephone number inside the kit.

- Antiseptic ointment/cream/solution; ask your vet's advice
- Rectal and/or ear thermometer
- Petroleum jelly and hydrogen peroxide (3 percent)
- Styptic pencil or powder
- Plastic eyedropper or syringe
- Sterile nonstick gauze pads
- Cotton balls and cotton swabs for the ears and around the eyes
- Bandages in two or three different widths

- Self-adhesive bandage
- Latex or rubber gloves
- Roll of narrow adhesive tape
- Scissors and tweezers—blunt, not pointed
- Potential tourniquet, e.g., a flat tape or cord
- Cold pack; keep one (or a small bag of peas) in the freezer. If you need to use it—for example, for a nose bleed or to reduce swelling—always wrap it well to avoid excessive chilling of tissue

Cat grass—Cats often like to chew on plants, and the sweet shoots of wheat grass are particularly appealing and safe. Although the benefits of eating grass are not fully understood, this does provide your cat with some roughage and may help with the coughing up of fur balls. Chewing cat grass will also provide your kitten with another activity and can help direct his attentions away from your other houseplants. "Cat grass" seeds can be bought from many pet and plant retailers and are easy to grow in pots that can be positioned around the home or even outside on the terrace or in the garden.

left: **A cat door will allow your kitten to move around freely into a safe outdoor enclosure.**

MAKING YOUR KITTEN FEEL AT HOME

Kittens need to spend time with their littermates and mother in order to learn good life skills. Animal shelters and some breeders are happy to home healthy kittens at approximately eight weeks of age. You'll often be responsible for all vaccinations that are required, although the kittens should have had health checks and some parasite treatments while they were still with the breeder.

Pedigree kittens are often slightly older when they are homed, per the recommendations of the major cat organizations. They're normally approximately 12 weeks old and have already had their full course of vaccinations. They will also have been wormed and treated for fleas.

left: **Vaccinations provide vital protection. The injections are quick and virtually painless.**

If you have reserved a kitten and will be collecting him at a later date, it is useful to give the breeder two blankets to put in with the mother and kittens. These will absorb the familiar scents of the litter and can be brought home when you do collect the kitten to help with the transition stage.

Welcoming Your Kitten

This is an exciting time, but remember that your kitten is going through a huge change and that he will take time to adjust. Your kitten will have experienced a number of things that could cause some stress: being taken from its littermates, traveling to your home, meeting new family members, and getting used to a new environment. Avoid overwhelming your kitten by making the transition quiet, calm, and pleasant. Luckily, young kittens can adjust very well and can quickly settle into their new lifestyle within a few weeks.

You will need to commit time to settling your new kitten in and building a bond of trust and affection. A young kitten is very energetic and will be keen to play and will love settling with you for a catnap. Create a routine from day one so that you ensure that your kitten is fed appropriately and is kept clean and contented. A happy, well-cared-for kitten will have a good chance to grow up healthy and problem free, so take time now to get it right. Good habits and a thorough socialization will make life with your cat extremely rewarding.

A good breeder will probably have taken the time to create a kitten pack for the new owner. This should include a diet sheet and advice about settling your kitten into your home.

Bringing Your New Kitten Home

Transport your kitten home in a secure cat carrier. Bring the carrier into the area where you want to keep your kitten. Gently place the cat carrier down in a safe, warm place and open the door. Let your kitten come out to explore in his own time. You can encourage this by sitting nearby and gently coaxing him with a familiar toy or titbit. Be prepared for this to take a little time depending on how stressful your kitten has found the journey.

Leave the cat carrier in the same place so that your kitten can retreat back to this safe spot if he feels worried. In time, your kitten will find new places to hide away and feel secure in, but until then the cat carrier will be an important refuge.

To help make your kitten feel more secure, lay

right: **Open the carrier and let your kitten out to explore slowly.**

left: **Play a fun game to encourage your kitten to develop confidence around you.**

below: **Make sure your kitten is familiar with the litter box location.**

out the blanket you brought back from the breeder, and keep noise and disturbance to a minimum. Some kittens settle well with a warmed cushion to comfort them.

As your kitten explores, carefully show him the litter box so he knows where to go when he needs to urinate or defecate. Don't move the box about, or your kitten may become confused and be forced to find an alternative toileting place.

right: **The familiar scents of your kitten's siblings and first bed can be brought home on a blanket. These help increase your kitten's security when he becomes part of the family.**

Providing a Safe Place

Restrict your kitten's movements around your home until he settles in. Choose a secure room or area where you can place the litter box, bedding, and food and water bowls. These need to be spaced apart, as cats dislike sleeping and eating near their toileting areas. Over time as your kitten's confidence grows, you'll be able to open up more areas of the house. Keep the doors and windows closed while your kitten is exploring. Be careful as kittens can move very quickly and can escape through tiny gaps.

Naming Your Pet

Picking a name for your kitten is fun, and everyone in your family will probably have suggestions. Choose a name that it easy to say. Cats respond well to certain sounds including words ending in the "ee" sound. Introduce your kitten's name by calling it and offering something fun or a tasty titbit as a reward when your kitten focuses his attention on you.

A kitten's stomach is walnut sized.

Establishing a Feeding Routine

Once your kitten has had a chance to settle in, he will probably feel like eating. Kittens eat small regular meals, and it's important that they eat a good diet. Place the food down and take note of what kind of appetite your kitten has. More detailed information about diet and feeding routines can be found on pages 34–41.

above: **All family members should get to bond with the kitten and help with his care.**

Setting Out-of-Bounds Areas

You may want to keep your kitten from going into certain areas in your home or being on certain items of furniture. These might include dangerous places or places you want to exclude just for reasons of hygiene. For instance:

- Kitchen work surfaces
- The dining table
- A baby's bedroom
- Near dangerous equipment

Kittens are adventurous and will happily climb up on furniture. Take care around unstable items that could topple, and ensure that bookcases, shelves, and radiators are securely fastened to the wall. Take care while carrying your kitten, as he can suddenly leap from your arms and may be injured if he falls to the ground.

Providing Day Care

If you work all day, you may choose to have a friend or family member come in to feed and tend to your kitten. You will need to give this person clear instructions about your kitten's feeding routine, how to clean the litter tray, and what games to play. You should leave your vet's number and address along with any instructions regarding any medical treatment.

Introducing an Identification Collar

There are some very good reasons to fit a collar, although each owner should think about why one would be useful. A collar can carry owner details, hold bells to scare away prey animals, and simply signal that this cat has an owner. A collar can also carry a message to inform other people that the cat is on a diet or has a medical problem and should not be offered food. Indoor and show cats do not often wear collars.

A collar will be totally foreign to your kitten, so it's important that you start to introduce it just for short periods before you begin to let the kitten outside. Since young kittens can easily wiggle out of a collar and are more likely to get caught up on one, it's suggested that five months is an appropriate age for a kitten to begin wearing one. Over time, your kitten will become used to the sensation and will forget about it. As

> **Expert Tip**
> Microchipping offers a permanent identification for your feline. It is a quick and virtually pain-free procedure that does not require a cat to be anesthe-tized. A vet uses a special needle to insert the microchip under your kitten's skin between the shoulder blades. The ID info on the chip can be accessed using a special wand device.

your kitten grows, you must of course remember to loosen the collar or change it for a larger one.

It is important to buy a collar specifically designed for cats because it will need to fit properly and release if your cat becomes caught up. Don't leave the collar too loose or it could easily slip and become stuck over your cat's jaw or foreleg. Both can cause serious distress and even injury.

Formulating Good Habits

- Create a routine so all the family members know and understand their role in caring for your kitten.
- Teach your children always to wash their hands after handling your kitten, especially before eating.

above: **A collar is a useful method of identification and should be paired with having your kitten microchipped.**

right **Your kitten needs to adjust to life away from his siblings.**

Introduction to the Family

Getting to know your new kitten is very exciting, but remember that a young animal can easily feel worried and anxious if he is exposed to lots of noise or movement. Your kitten needs to have a chance to familiarize himself with his environment before meeting lots of people.

Try to observe the following rules to make sure your kitten can relax:

- Everyone should move slowly and carefully around him.
- Sit down when first meeting and petting the kitten.
- Let your kitten approach you in his own time.
- Children should be asked to sit on the floor before the kitten is brought in and should be dissuaded from carrying the kitten around.
- Talk calmly and quietly until your kitten is accustomed to you and your voice.
- Always supervise children when they are with your kitten.

Handling your kitten—Kittens are very fragile and can break bones easily, so it's important to handle them carefully. Take care while moving around, since kittens can easily trip you up or get stepped on, especially if you're not used to having a pet underfoot.

When you lift your kitten, do so slowly and make sure he's supported well. Whizzing him up into the air in a rush may frighten him and could make him resist being picked up in the future. Always pick up a kitten by supporting his bottom and chest. This is much more

> **Safety Tip**
> Don't pick up your kitten by the scruff of the neck; support his weight gently but securely with both hands instead.

comfortable than lifting him by the middle where his tummy could be squashed. Kittens often struggle and wiggle about if restrained. Be gentle and gradually let your kitten get used to being held. If your kitten feels secure, he is apt to be happier to remain longer in your arms.

Introducing your new baby—Cats and babies can live together safely if proper precautions are taken. Good hygiene is sensible with all pets and if your kitten is kept up to date with his vaccinations and parasite prevention, there's little health risk to a young child.

Being prepared will allow your kitten to adapt to your new arrival with a minimum of stress. Prior to the baby's arrival home, identify any out-of-bounds areas so your feline won't suddenly feel displaced when the baby arrives. Allow your kitten to explore the new items brought into the house ready for the baby. Recognize that you will probably spend less time with your kitten once the baby comes home. All kittens need attention, but if yours is particularly attached and wants to be with you throughout the day, then it may be upsetting for him to be suddenly pushed away when you bring your new baby home.

left: **Children must be gentle and support the kitten when lifting.**

After the birth, bring home a blanket smelling of your baby from the hospital and allow your kitten to sniff it. It is also important to introduce the sounds of children early on; ideally, this should be part of a kitten's socialization experiences. If you don't know any children who might be persuaded to visit you, then use a sound effects CD to expose your kitten to the noises.

Once home, you should sit down with the infant and allow your kitten to approach you. As with any new experience, don't force your kitten to come any closer than he wants. Kittens like to snuggle up to mom and baby for warmth and comfort and they rarely cause any problems. Some will bond so closely that they become very protective of their new family member.

below: **Always supervise young children around your kitten. Kittens are fragile and may scratch or bite if scared.**

below: **Pleasant social experiences with children are important and will make your kitten calmer and happier around them in the future.**

Safety Tip

Cats can carry the toxoplasmosis parasite *(Toxoplasma gondii)*, which is then shed in the cat's feces. This parasite can affect humans, too; it can pass from a pregnant mother to her unborn child, who may develop signs of infection later in life. Good hygiene is essential, and pregnant women should avoid cleaning litter boxes or should wear rubber gloves when doing so. Cover children's play areas and sandpits in between playtime, as cats may use them as bathroom areas.

Introducing Your Kitten to Family Pets

Your small kitten can be easily scared or hurt by larger pets when he first comes home. But cats are natural hunters and also have the ability to hurt smaller pets. Introduce everyone in the family household carefully.

Get into good habits from the beginning. How your existing pets respond to your new kitten depends on their previous experience of young cats, their own social abilities, and, in the case of dogs, their level of training.

Meeting another cat—Although young cats are more readily accepted than older ones, some cats can be extremely upset when a new kitten is brought into their home territory.

Let your kitten settle in within his safe room before you try introducing the cats. Some very friendly, laid-back cats can be introduced quite quickly, but getting the

above: **Rushing a kitten's introduction can create stress and tension for both cats, so take your time to ensure amicable relations.**

meeting right makes things much easier. Here are some tips to a good start:

- Try creating a familiar group scent by rubbing both cats with a slightly damp towel.
- Introduce the cats during quieter, sleepy times.
- The kitten can remain safely in his carrier or a pet crate so your resident cat gets used to seeing him without being able to chase him.
- Give your older cat praise and rewards when the kitten is present. The original pet can feel unsettled by the sudden loss of attention and from having to share with the new arrival.

Make sure that you make time for your older pets but also make sure that some of this occurs when the kitten is present to help build good associations.

- Take your time and be patient while they grow accustomed to one another.
- Supervise all contact until you are sure both cats are relaxed in one another's presence.
- If severe aggression continues, you may have to accept that your original cat is not suited to living with others and consequently re-home the kitten. This is the fairest option.

Meeting your dog—Take care, as even a friendly dog can hurt a kitten while playing.

- Child gates should be fitted before you bring your kitten home so that the dog can be excluded from an area if you so choose.
- Provide your kitten with escape routes wherever he roams in the house.
- Keep your dog on a lead when you make the introductions. Keep your dog busy with his favorite game or treat.
- Place your kitten in a window perch or cat tree so that he can observe the dog safely from an elevated surface.
- Swap scents between the animals using a cloth rubbed over both pets.

Keeping Small Pets Safe

- Make sure that all cages and tanks are secure and cannot be tipped over by an energetic kitten.
- Don't allow your kitten to rest on the top of cages, as this could cause the smaller pets to feel severe anxiety and could be dangerous. Cats are often attracted to the warm lids over fish tanks or by the movements of the fish below, but this is dangerous if the lid collapses into the tank, especially if there is an electric light or heater attached to it.
- Don't allow your young children to handle small pets around your kitten; a hamster or gerbil, for example, could easily be caught and killed if it is accidentally dropped.

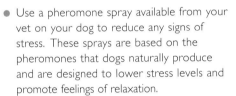

- Use a pheromone spray available from your vet on your dog to reduce any signs of stress. These sprays are based on the pheromones that dogs naturally produce and are designed to lower stress levels and promote feelings of relaxation.
- Never force your cat to meet your dog.

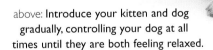

above: **Introduce your kitten and dog gradually, controlling your dog at all times until they are both feeling relaxed.**

- If your dog is determined to chase or attack your kitten despite all your training, you may have to consider the practical and safety implications of keeping the kitten. It may be kinder to rehome him.

left: **Some adult cats react aggressively toward an unfamiliar kitten, so don't leave them together unsupervised.**

DAILY LIFE

Kittens are renowned for being active and playful, but you may not know that play activity is actually very important in your kitten's development. This is the time when kittens will practice and perfect the movements, agility, and hunting skills that they would need as adults if they were living in the wild.

Safety Tip
Never leave your kitten alone with a feather wand or string toy, as he could become tangled up in it, choke on the string, or ingest it, requiring surgical removal.

Kittens will start to show play and predatory activity within the first few weeks of life and will practice their skills on their siblings and various items in their surrounding environment. Letting him be active is important in terms of keeping your kitten healthy and happy.

Your kitten has a natural desire to follow his feline instincts to pounce, swipe, jump, and capture prey and will be happiest if he can fulfil these needs within his life as a pet. Each kitten will have different needs depending upon his breed and genetic makeup. A single kitten will need more intensive play time with you than will one who can frolic and wrestle with a feline friend regularly during the day.

Reducing Problem Behavior

Playing with your new kitten will help him use up energy and will reduce the chances of the kitten focusing his attention in an unwelcome way on your furniture or possessions. Without being adequately mentally stimulated, your kitten may develop frustrations that can lead to behavior problems as he grows.

A shy cat can often be enticed to play if the right toy is found. Over time, this helps build up his confidence and enjoyment in interactions with his owner.

Giving a younger cat opportunities to express his instincts and use up some excess energy in the pursuit of playthings will also allow any older, more frail cats in the house a reprieve from being knocked around and generally distressed.

Good Relationships

Playtime is also a perfect opportunity for you to bond with your kitten and teach him about appropriate ways to interact with you. Always encourage your kitten to play with toys rather than your hands, feet, or clothing. Otherwise, your kitten could grow up continuing to grab and pounce on hands and feet. This becomes a problem when your cat is fully grown and using teeth and claws in this rough game. Everyone in the family should be consistent in playing only appropriate games or your kitten may become confused about what is acceptable.

Set aside time to play with your kitten several times a day. However, try not to respond to demanding behavior. If you do, your kitten will become more and more attention seeking as he learns how to get you to respond to his wishes. Provide him with plenty of toys that he can play with independently.

Toys That Kittens Find Entertaining

Kittens and cats like toys that allow them to perform natural behaviors. They love toys that mimic prey in their shape or movements, so small furry or feathered toys are often favorites. Provision of a variety of toys is essential so that your kitten can find entertainment no matter what his mood may be. Varying the toys is important so that they stay novel and interesting. You should regularly put some away while bringing others out to play with. Wand toys are fun for kittens since you can control the movements to suit your kitten's age and ability.

left: **The majority of young cats will play with a toy that's being wiggled and jiggled about by their owner. Wand toys keep claws safely out of the way of hands.**

Feathers are a favorite for many cats.

Safety Considerations

Replace any toy that has begun to deteriorate and may be dangerous. Supervise your kitten when he is playing with toys with strings or ribbons that could be swallowed or become caught around the legs or the neck.

below right: **Children should use toys rather than hands or feet when playing with their kitten.**

above: **Feline play involves hunting-type actions. Toys provide a suitable outlet for these natural instincts.**

Litter Box Habits

Cats can be very particular about their toileting preferences, so this aspect of their lives needs some thought and understanding. Your kitten will need a litter box available from day one, and preferably two if you have a multilevel home.

Young kittens can be perfectly litter-trained by the time they are brought home; as long as early routines are established, you can avoid many problems. Kittens learn by observing their mother. The occasional kitten that has not had an ideal upbringing may be confused about where to toilet or anxious about using a litter box. When your kitten first arrives home, take him to the litter box so that he knows where to go. Take your kitten there after he eats and after he wakes from sleeping.

Accessing the litter box—Place the litter box in a position that is easy for your kitten to get to. Your home will seem very large to your new kitten, and he cannot be expected to know how to make his way through many rooms to find the litter box. For this reason it is best to keep your kitten in your chosen, prepared area for the first few weeks. Supervise your kitten if you allow him more freedom around your home. If he's caught short, he may find another place to toilet.

When you do start to allow your kitten to move freely around your home, you should stay vigilant and remember to take your kitten back to the litter box often. Providing more than one is essential and can help prevent your kitten from being caught short. The position of the litter box is important to get right, or your kitten may be forced to go and find a more convenient place.

Locating a litter box—Ideally, a box should:
- Be located in a quiet area (not where there are too many comings and goings involving family members).
- Be available all day (not in a room or basement that's shut during the day or at night).
- Away from windows or glass doors where your kitten may feel insecure.

Not every kitten that starts to use a litter box will cover up his feces, so don't panic. This depends on observational learning from the mother, the type, the amount of litter being used, and the kitten's confidence.

Cleaning the litter box—You'll need to begin cleaning out the litter box after its first use. Clean out at least the soiled litter, if not the entire contents of the box. Cats are highly fastidious and don't like soiled litter. Get into a good cleaning routine to prevent unpleasant odors from building up or to prevent your kitten's wanting to find an alternative bathroom area because he finds the box unappealing. Hot water and detergent are normally ideal for cleaning the plastic pan, since many cleaning products that smell very

A cat's sensitive nose will detect a soiled box.

above: **Cats dislike waiting to toilet, which can be a problem if several are sharing one litter box.**

strongly will actually deter use—or may be toxic to cats.

If you own several cats, you should provide more than one box. A good rule is to provide one litter box per cat plus an extra one. The litter boxes should be located on different levels in the home and not all in a line. Select a small litter box for a kitten and larger ones with high sides for adult cats.

Expert Tip
If your cat needs to be medicated, don't be tempted to grab him while he is using the litter box. He may be easier to catch at this time, but there's a strong chance that you'll upset his routine and unintentionally created negative associations with the litter box. He may begin to avoid using it.

Hygiene is important when cleaning boxes.

right: **Your kitten may eliminate outdoors if you allow supervised outings.**

Cat Carriers

A cat carrier is an essential piece of equipment for all cat owners. Despite the fact that you may not use it very often, it is still important to have a secure way to transport your cat in case of emergency or when traveling for his health checks.

Having to search around for a carrier during an emergency will cause more panic and could create a critical time delay for an ill or injured cat.

Choosing a cat carrier—
When choosing a cat carrier, consider the design aspects that will help make your cat feel relaxed and safe. The right carrier should make transporting your kitten to the vet, to cat shows, or on family trips a much more pleasant event for you both. There are carriers available to suit most budgets, and the style you choose will depend upon how often you intend to transport your cat. Show cats will need a larger carrier with feeding and drinking facilities since they are likely to spend much longer periods traveling.

Here are some points to consider:
- Is the carrier secure? Carriers often come with lockable doors, but many have simple catches or buckles to prevent the door from opening and releasing your cat. Make sure you know how these work and replace a carrier with broken catches.
- Will your cat feel safe? Being enclosed helps a cat feel more secure, so avoid a carrier with open bars on all sides. A carrier with a view out of one end is ideal.

- Can you get your cat inside the carrier? Hard-to-handle cats may be easier to put in via a top-opening door. This will also provide your vet with a better way of getting your cat out than having to tip the carrier up on its end. Make sure the carrier you choose is large enough to hold your cat safely.
- Can you lift and carry the carrier fairly easily? Some brands, especially those with more built-in features, are rather heavy. Some come with a strong shoulder strap; others should have a strong handle.

Preparing the carrier—
Leave your carrier in your kitten's own environment so it begins to smell familiar. The door should be open so that your kitten can sniff and enter it in his own time. If you have a nervous kitten, don't approach him while he's investigating the carrier.

Here are some helpful hints:
- Hide tasty treats inside the carrier each day for your kitten to discover.
- Once your kitten is comfortable going into the carrier, practice closing the door for a minute or two while he eats the treats.
- Be patient! It can take cats some time to investigate new items, but it will happen eventually.
- Wash off any vet smells from the carrier after a visit, and place your cat's bedding inside to make the carrier seem welcoming.
- Feline pheromone spray makes a carrier seem more familiar and can ease the stress associated with traveling in a carrier.

Tips While Traveling

- Placing paper towels underneath the bedding can help absorb any accidents that may occur during your journey.
- Prevent the carrier from bouncing or spinning as you move it from the house to your vehicle.
- Secure the carrier with seat belts in the back seat so it cannot tip or rock as the car accelerates and decelerates.
- Avoid putting the carrier in front passenger seat because the cat may be injured if a collision occurs and the air bag is deployed.
- Do not open the carrier during your journey or once inside the waiting room at the veterinary clinic.
- Don't drag or tip your cat out. Open the top of the carrier instead and gently lift your kitten out.

right: **Support the carrier securely to steady it and limit its movements.**

below: **A calm traveler makes a calmer vet patient.**

above and below: **Carriers should be secure places for your kitten. Familiar items of bedding and pheromone sprays can help reduce stress.**

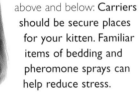

DIET AND NUTRITION

Getting your kitten's diet right is important so that she can grow properly and remain in good health. Sadly, cats are becoming increasingly obese as a result of over-feeding, which can lead to such health issues as arthritis, heart problems, and diabetes.

A cat would naturally eat small prey animals.

Your kitten is physically designed to be a predator and is an *obligate carnivore*. This means that she has evolved and adapted to survive on a meat-based diet. Cats actually require very little nutrition from other sources of food such as plants. *A cat cannot survive on a vegetarian diet.*

Your kitten's ancestors survived by catching and consuming small prey animals like rodents and birds. This natural cat diet is balanced and contains very low amounts of fat and carbohydrates. Evolution has specialized your cat's digestion so she has optimal biochemical mechanisms for breaking down proteins.

Feeding Behavior

Your kitten will develop eating habits while she is young. Kittens learn about food preferences from their mother through observation and from foods or prey she may bring to them. Young kittens have an exploratory nature and will happily test out small amounts of new foods. Introducing new foods becomes harder and takes longer as the cat ages. Normally, cats eat enough to give them the amount of calories they need for their normal energy expenditure. High-calorie diets may cause problems if the cat gets into the habit of consuming too much while living a sedentary lifestyle.

The easiest way to provide your kitten with all the required nutrients is to choose a quality commercial diet. Work with your veterinarian to select the right diet that best meets your feline's age, health, and activity level. Many cats, like humans, get used to eating a fatty diet and then turn their noses up at healthier options. However, to ensure a long, healthy life, it is important that your cat eats a balanced diet.

Naturally, cats would hunt small prey animals and so are designed to ingest small meals. Ideally, your pet cat should eat around three small meals a day rather than being given a large bowl filled with food at a single meal.

Physical Design

Cats are much better at digesting animal proteins than plant-based products. You need to identify foods based on plant protein (such as grain), as opposed to animal protein, because the type of protein is critical to the quality of the food. This is possible by reading the ingredients label on the can or bag that identifies the type of protein present.

Feeding a Balanced Diet

Professional opinion suggests that quality wet (or canned) food provides the best nutritional source for pet cats. Cats fed only dry food can suffer from chronic, low-level dehydration, which can lead

> **Expert Tip**
> Don't feed your kitten table scraps, as you'll only encourage her to beg and demand food while you are eating your meal.

to kidney and bladder problems. For convenience and variation, many owners feed both canned and dry food. If your cat has any health problems, your vet will be able to advise you about the most suitable diet.

Read the label and choose a food that it based on animal protein, not a plant protein (grain). Factual information about the contents of the diet are listed in the product information panel. Don't be swayed by glamorous marketing strategies and sweeping claims in the ads, as these can be misleading.

Feeding Routine

Like most young animals, kittens require more regular feeding than adult cats do. Your kitten needs to eat enough food to grow and maintain a healthy weight and to have optimal energy. The life stage of your cat will determine how much this is.

General Feed Guidelines

The amount of food you should feed your kitten will depend greatly upon her breed and the type of diet you have chosen. A Persian kitten will have a different appetite from a Bengal due to the differences in their activity levels. Your chosen brand will give a guideline that you can follow according to your kitten's weight, which you should check once a week. Adjust her food if necessary. Split the

above: **Dry food is a nutritious and convenient way to feed your kitten in between wet meals.**

recommended daily amount into the meals shown on the chart below left.

It normally works well to free-feed some dry food during the day and to provide set meals of canned food. Healthy, happy cats will normally eat a little food every few hours. However, some will gorge themselves if left to their own devices, so set mealtimes to control portions and prevent obesity. This often occurs in cats who lack mental and physical stimulation during their day. Remember that adult cats will require fewer calories than will a growing adolescent.

below: **While she is small, your kitten will enjoy eating a little food several times a day, rather than two or three larger meals.**

2–3 months: 4 meals per day
3–5 months: 3 meals per day
6–12 months: 2–3 meals per day
Adults: 2+ meals per day

Offer fresh food daily.

35

Feeding a Balanced Diet

The components of a balanced diet are water, protein, essential fatty acids, minerals and vitamins, and carbohydrates (for energy).

Water—This is absolutely critical to all cats. Without water, your cat would not survive for long. In the wild, cats would naturally ingest a lot of water with their natural diet. This would have provided a survival advantage to the cat's ancestors which lived in dry environments. Household cats often don't seem to drink very much, which can be a concern. Make sure your cat has fresh, clean water available at all times. Remember that diet, health, and environmental temperature will influence how much water your cat needs to drink.

Protein—Animal protein is critical for growth and maintenance of bone, muscle, and ligaments. It's also involved in hormonal, neurotransmitter, and enzyme activity.

Fats—The right amount allows the absorption of some vitamins, provides essential fatty acids, and also provides energy. Fat helps keep the coat glossy and the skin in good condition.

Vitamins and minerals—These are required for the enzymatic processes needed for energy release, body function, and growth. Essential minerals are iron, copper, potassium, zinc, manganse, selenium, and iodine.

Carbohydrates—These provide fuel that converts to energy. Cats would not naturally eat the amounts of carbohydrates found in

Expert Tip
Many cats are intolerant to cow's milk and suffer from diarrhea if they drink it. Buy special lactose-free milk if you want to occasionally treat your pet.

many commercial foods since they don't produce the right enzymes to break down carbohydrates as effectively as we can.

Additives—Nonessentials, these are added to your cat's food by the manufacturer. This is to increase the food's shelf life and to make it taste better. The same additives are used in human food.

Dietary fiber—Fiber doesn't feature much in a natural feline diet, although it is present in many commercially prepared diets, especially those designed to give a feeling of fullness for cats who are obese or have weight issues. However, one disadvantage of high-fiber foods is the fact that they can increase the amount of water passed in the feces.

Never serve your cat a commercial diet designed for dogs. Your cat requires different nutrients to stay healthy. For example, without adequate amounts of taurine, which is found in a meat-based diet, your cat may become seriously ill.

left: **Kittens grow very quickly and so require a good-quality diet.**

Food Type Pros and Cons

Wet Food	Canned	• Approximately 80 percent water • Contains protein, such as beef, fish, chicken • Usually higher in protein than dry foods • Protein content normally meat-based • Tends to deliver an irresistible aroma to encourage cats to eat
	Moist	• Contains between 20 and 40 percent water • Usually available in convenient packaging, including single-serving size • Similar ingredients to dry food and generally contains less protein than canned food
Dry Food	Kibble	• Contains protein and carbohydrates, such as wheat and oats • Approximately 6 to 10 percent water • Contains up to 50 percent carbohydrates • Protein often plant-based • Tends to be less expensive per meal than canned food • Convenient to feed and easy to store
Homemade	Diet of cooked meat, chicken, and fish	• Careful recipe plan important for optimum nutrition • Time-consuming to prepare • Adding calcium, taurine, and vitamin supplements may be necessary • Can contain good-quality meat • Often more expensive

left: Adult cats require different nutritional needs than growing kittens do. Gradually switch to an adult diet when your kitten is one year of age.

Other Dietary Considerations

Choosing a diet for your kitten can be confusing as there seem to be so many good options available. The best type for you and your kitten might not be immediately obvious, so consider the following factors to ensure ease in selecting a diet that is consistently good for your kitten.

A healthy, growing kitten should have a good appetite.

Cost— Finding a good food that is affordable is important. The cost of cat food can be slightly deceptive. Lower-quality products need to be eaten in higher amounts to provide adequate nutrients, so you could actually end up buying more to achieve the same nutritional result. Cheap foods may not be nutritious for your cat and could lead to expensive health problems later on. Ask your vet about the type of food best for your kitten as she grows.

Storage—Canned food has a long shelf life. Dry food should be stored in a self-sealing bag or plastic container to prevent it from becoming damp, stale, or accessible to pests, such as mice. Find a convenient place to store the food you buy in your kitchen, utility room or shed. Make sure the food is used by its sell-by date, so put newer packs in the back of the cupboard.

Purchase—Choose a brand that you can buy relatively easily. Suddenly running out and being forced to change to another brand could cause digestive upset to your kitten. Commercial food can be ordered through your vet, local pet supply store, or online via the Internet. Make sure you re-order in plenty of time, and ensure that you have stocked up adequately before leaving your kitten with a pet sitter.

Hygiene—Open cans or containers of canned food could become rancid, smell, and attract insects. Bacteria will multiply extremely quickly on the surfaces of the packets or the bowls. Although most cats are fairly resistant, this could cause young kittens or elderly or immune-suppressed cats to become ill. It also poses a hygiene risk to the humans and other animals in the home. Bowls and scoops will require daily cleaning. Wash them in hot soapy water and thoroughly rinse them, or wash them in your dishwasher.

Understanding Food Labels

Choosing from among all the different commercial brands of cat food and weighing their claims can be confusing. There are no real scientific differences between some of the advertised types, such as Premium, Natural, or Lite, so you are best to look at the exact product contents before making your decision. More confusion may arise when deciding on how much to feed your cat. Each cat's caloric requirements depend on her age, health, and levels of activity. The label will give you a guideline, but you will need to be

left: **Growing kittens require more calories than fully grown cats do.**

Kibble can be used as a treat for some kittens.

Food can be used for training and be hidden within some toys, as well as being delivered via your kitten's bowl.

responsible for deciding the correct amount to feed your own cat. You can discuss your queries with your vet if you are concerned that your cat is eating too little or too much.

Comparing Ingredients

Comparing food labels is difficult because different products contain different amounts of water. To make an accurate comparison, you need to compare the dry weight contents to determine exactly what levels of ingredients are present. Luckily this isn't as daunting as it seems, and it is quite a simple calculation to make.

Read your label: it may, for example, say something like 80 percent water, 6 percent protein, 3 percent fat. We know there must be 20 percent dry matter in this product since 80 percent is water. Begin by dividing the amount of the listed nutrients by the amount of dry matter.

Protein: $6/20 = 0.3$
Fat: $3/20 = 0.15$

To calculate the percentage of the ingredient, multiply the figures you have obtained by 100.

Protein: 0.3×100
Fat: 0.15×100

There is 30 percent protein and 15 percent fat in this example.

Energy Content

Energy or "kcal" (standing for kilocalorie, or just calorie) is the amount of energy available from your cat's food. Energy is required for the body to function, for physical exertion, and for efficient temperature regulation. Each cat will therefore have a slightly different energy usage.

left: **Read the label carefully when choosing foods for your kitten.**

Changing the Recommended Diet

Once your kitten has settled into her new home, you can gradually change to your chosen diet. Do this slowly or you risk causing a digestive upset. Make the switch over a period of two weeks.

Each kitten will take to the change differently, depending upon her background and prior experience. Be patient and remember that cats may be hesitant to try new foods.

Safety Tip
Don't allow your cat to go without food for more than 24 hours. Feed only small amounts of the original food so your cat is still hungry enough to try the new food.

right: Small amounts of new foods can be given safely, but switch to a new diet slowly to prevent digestive upsets.

Food-Switching Suggestions

- Stop free-feeding food until the exchange of brands has been made. Set regular meal times to encourage your cat to eat at a consistent time.

- Take uneaten food away after 1 hour.

- Slightly warmed food may titillate your cat's taste buds.

- Sprinkle some of the old food on top of the new diet. Crush up the original dry food to prevent your kitten from selecting only those kibble pieces.

- Be prepared to phase in the switch over many weeks if necessary.

- Make sure your cat is fed in a safe place so she feels totally relaxed.

Supplements—A good-quality diet should provide your kitten with the necessary vitamins and minerals. However, owners looking to enhance their cat's coat may also feed certain feline supplements. Do not give cod liver oil, as this can contain grossly excessive amounts of vitamin A. Too many vitamins can cause serious health problems, so always ask your vet before adding a supplement, and select only products designed for cats.

Eating Problems

Overeating—High-energy diets or low-stimulation environments may result in a cat continuing to eat, despite having her caloric needs satisfied. Obesity is becoming a serious problem among domestic cats, and veterinary treatments for diseases relating to excess weight are on the increase. Cats fed on a good meat diet will not require large amounts of additional dry food.

Not eating—If your cat hasn't eaten for a day and cannot be enticed with her favorite foods, take her to the vet. Reasons for lack of appetite vary from illness to dental problems, so it's best to get the cause properly diagnosed.

Typical Weight Ranges

Small cats	7 pounds snd under
Medium cats (including your average mixed breed)	Between 8 and 12 pounds
Large cats	More than 12 pounds

below left: **The correct amount of food required depends upon your cat. Large, energetic cats will use up more energy than smaller, more lethargic individuals, who will gain weight more easily.**

right: **Size differences between kittens become more apparent as each week passes.**

Don't let your small kitten become an overweight cat.

left: **Monitor your kitten's growth by weighing regularly and keeping a record of the results. A saggy stomach, double chin, and hard-to-detect ribs are telltale signs of excess weight.**

Ideal Weights

The size range of cats is actually quite small when you compare them to other pets like dogs. However, there definitely is still a healthy range for your cat, and it will benefit you both to maintain this. Your vet will be able to help and advise you about the ideal weight for your particular cat since they vary among individuals. Many owners don't notice the weight creeping on. However, maintaining the correct weight is ultimately for the well-being of your pet.

Male cats are typically heavier than females. If you are concerned about weight gain, then discuss with your vet so you can rule out a medical cause. Then, ask how you can fine-tune your cat's feeding and exercise regimen to achieve an ideal weight.

Here are some tips for maintaining ideal weight:
- Feed a high-quality diet.
- Provide only suitably sized portions.
- Encourage your cat to be active for at least 20 minutes a day.
- Be consistent in your feeding and playing habits.

YOUR KITTEN'S HEALTH

Ensuring that your kitten grows up in ideal condition is naturally important, so you should arrange regular health checks with your vet. You will be the person most likely to notice any changes or problems, so getting into good habits early and knowing what to look out for is important.

Set your young kitten up for a healthy life by providing her with the necessary care. Although the mother will pass on some immunity to her kittens, they still  need extra protection against serious infections. Discuss your kitten's vaccinations with your vet, who will be able to advise you on the best course for you.

Finding a Vet

Your kitten needs a veterinarian just as you  benefit by having a family physician. Don't wait for a problem to occur. Ask your friends for recommendations of vets in your area. Some people and cats prefer feline-only clinics, but the main issue is whether you and your cat will feel comfortable and get the treatment required. Go in and chat with the staff about the services they offer.

Many people have their vets check a new kitten once she's had a chance to settle in. If you are ever concerned about your kitten's health, then seek veterinary advice quickly. Problems are always easier to treat during their early stages, and you could save yourself a lot of worry, too.

Daily Checks

Spending some time every day petting and observing your cat will allow you to spot any problems. You will notice any injuries and pick up on weepy eyes or a runny nose before these problems become serious. Ask yourself if your kitten is eating, drinking, and behaving normally. Regular, gentle handling will help teach your kitten to tolerate being examined or groomed and will improve her confidence around people.

Vets advise that owners should clean their cat's teeth daily to reduce the likelihood of tartar buildup. While some owners have success with a kitty toothbrush, most find that putting cat toothpaste on a rubber thimble is easier to run along a kitten's teeth than using a toothbrush is. Your kitten may chew on the thimble and improve your cleaning ability. Encouraging your cat to chew on appropriate foods, such as dental treats, will help maintain gum health. Remember, you play a role in maintaining your cat's healthy teeth and gums. Getting into a dental habit at home can save you money on professional dental cleaning that requires your cat to be anesthetized.

Weekly Checks

Checking your cat from head to toe on a regular basis will allow you to know what's normal and what's not. Begin at the head, checking eyes, mouth, and ears, and then move back, running your hands gently over the body. Remember that cats will quietly cover up many problems. If you notice that your cat is quieter than normal or, if her eating or toileting habits have changed, pay a visit to your vet just in case a problem is developing.

Monthly Checks

Get into the habit of checking your kitten's nail length and trimming the tips with suitable nail cutters on a monthly basis.

Summer Risks	Winter Risks
• Hyperthermia (heatstroke) • Fleas breed faster during warmer seasons • Sunburn: Pale and white cats are particularly vulnerable to ear and nose carcinomas • Being shut inside a car is highly dangerous • Gardeners spray pesticides on their plants, which could be toxic to your cat	• Hypothermia (exposure to cold) • Cats may seek warmth inside a car's engine and may be injured if you drive off inadvertently • The dry air inside a home may dry out a cat's coat or cause static electricity • Antifreeze spills on the garage floor can be lethal to cats if ingested

left: **Brush your kitten's teeth regularly to prevent dental problems.**

above: **Seasonal changes can bring dangers such as hypothermia or frost-bite caused by cold.**

left: **Use a cat-wipe or tissue to clean your kitten's eyes by wiping gently outward.**

Yearly Health Checks

It is important that all cats, regardless of their lifestyle, have annual vet checkups to ensure that any physical changes are identified. Your vet will be able to advise you about weight changes and the best diets to suit different ages and can inform you about other suitable products.

Your vet will also be able to advise you about the best vaccination course for you, taking into account the area in which you live and your personal circumstances. It is possible to have your cat's blood tested to check for antibody levels if you are unsure about whether to vaccinate each year. However, the results are not as strongly correlated to the prevention of infection as regular booster vaccinations are.

If your kitten will venture outside or mix with other cats, it is recommended that you make sure she has protection against the serious and potentially fatal diseases shown in the table below.

Diseases with No Vaccine Protection

Feline immunodeficiency virus (FIV)—This viral disease, commonly known as feline AIDS, weakens the immune system. No vaccine has been developed to date. It can be spread via cat

Disease		Symptoms	Comments
Feline infectious enteritis (FIE)		Vomiting and diarrhea	Severe physical effects which can be fatal
Feline calicivirus (FCV) and Feline herpes virus (FHV-1) (cat flu)		Sneezing, mucus running from nose and eyes, ulceration of tongue	May have lifelong adverse effects. Kittens and old cats are most vulnerable
Feline leukemia virus (FeLV)		Attacks the immune system and may affect either the red or white blood cells or result in tumors	Kittens are highly vulnerable. Infection is lifelong and is usually fatal within 3 years
	Bordetella bronchiseptica	Respiratory problems similar to kennel cough	Particularly troublesome to kittens
	Rabies	Changes in behavior result from nervous system damage; intensive aggression follows before the cat becomes paralyzed	Fatal disease that can be passed to humans; there is no cure
Feline chlamydophilosis		Inflamed eyes, breathing problems	Spread through direct contact between cats, so vaccination may not always be necessary; can be treated with antibiotics

Expert Tip
Cats can purr even when they are in pain, so don't ignore other symptoms just because your kitten sounds happy.

bites, and through blood transfusions, and mother cats can transmit this virus. A carrier cat can be successfully homed as a single cat and may not show the disease until the cat is older.

Feline infectious peritonitis (FIP)—Caused by a feline coronavirus, this disease has varied symptoms and is easily passed between cats living together. To date, treatments have had limited effect and prognosis is often poor.

Feline infectious anemia (FIA)—This is an infection that is more serious in senior cats or those who are already carrying FIV or FeLV. FIA may be transmitted via flea infestation, bites, or scratches between cats.

Luckily, advances in medicine are always being made, and some of these problems may have better treatments in the near future. When blood testing for FeLV, FIV, and FIP, you should request repeat tests to rule out false positive results.

above: **Your kitten should complete her vaccinations to ensure protection from disease.**

below **Annual checkups with, your vet help keep your cat healthy.**

Your vet will advise you about all aspects of your kitten's health.

Parasite Prevention and Protection

It is possible to prevent parasite infestation of your kitten by regular preventative treatment. Parasite control is particularly important in cats with access to the outdoors. Your vet will be able to advise you on the most appropriate course of action for your cat. Use only products specifically designed for cats.

Types of parasitic worm—Prevention of worms is critical, as you often won't be able to tell if your cat has become infested until the problem is severe. Most worms are contracted from eating prey animals.

Tapeworm: These flat worms live in the intestines. You may spot telltale white rice-size particles clustered around your cat's anus. These are body segments that have been passed in the cat's feces. Eggs are released from them and humans and other animals may be infected by them.

Roundworm (left): These spaghettilike worms are found in the intestines. Your cat's health may deteriorate despite her eating well. Vomiting and diarrhea may also occur. Humans and other species can contract roundworm since the eggs are passed out into the cat's environment.

Fleas and Ticks—Many varieties of fleas can feed on your kitten's blood. These can bite both animal and human members of the family, resulting in inflamed bite areas. Indeed, a single flea bite can trigger off a highly unpleasant reaction in some cats. The skin becomes itchy and sore, causing the cat to scratch excessively and lose hair. You will be able to see telltale flea-dirt in your kitten's coat, which consists primarily of dried blood. Veterinary treatment is often necessary if secondary infections set in or if the scratching requires an antihistamine treatment.

There are four stages in a flea's life cycle: egg, larva, pupa, and adult. It takes 15 days for a flea to develop from egg to adult, although it can lie dormant in suboptimum conditions and may last months between meals.

Ticks—These are part of the arachnid family (as are mites), and they feed on blood. They are seasonal and will be more prevalent in certain areas. Ticks can transmit many diseases and parasites that can affect humans and cats alike, so it's important to use effective products to deter them. Fully engorged female ticks look like swollen raisins attached to the skin.

There are four stages in a tick life cycle: egg, larva, nymph, and adult. Each stage feeds upon a host animal before dropping off to develop further. It will

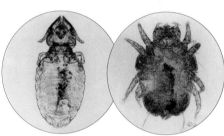

above: **Lice cause scratchy skin which often becomes flaky and dry.**

above: **Cheyletiella mites cause irritating dermatitis on the back, neck, and head.**

then climb up onto vegetation and wait for a new host animal to brush past, allowing it to attach itself to the skin. Ticks are often found around the cat's ears and eyes.

Mites—Several types of mites may be interested in your kitten.

the chemical Permethrin on cats. Permethrin is commonly found in dog flea treatments, but it is highly toxic to cats, which may die from exposure to this insecticide. Don't administer parasite treatments more often than stated on the label, as this also could be toxic. Seek advice from your vet if your kitten still has a parasite problem.

Fleas can be particularly hard to control, so use a product that repels new fleas as well as killing any already present. Remember to treat all the pets in your home, as well as all bedding and soft furnishings, if you've had an infestation.

Ear mites: These can invade your cat's ear canals, but may reside on other areas of the body. Ear mites are very contagious and spread between different pets in the household, especially if they share bedding or groom one another. Symptoms include scratching and shaking of the head.

Harvest mites (chiggers): These mites are very common in certain areas and look like tiny red dots, often infecting a cat's ears.

Demodex mites: These mites are more common in cats with a suppressed immune system and cause hair loss around the head and face areas. The skin becomes itchy and inflamed.

Treatments—A number of products have been designed to combat a range of internal and external parasites including spot-on applications, topical powders, shampoo sprays, dips, and fogs. The suitability of each product varies, so check the label. Avoid using products containing

below: **You should apply parasite treatments at home on a regular basis to prevent outbreaks of infestation.**

Flea treatments that once required sprays are now applied directly to the skin between the shoulders

Disposable gloves will protect your skin.

ROUTINE GROOMING

Although cats normally spend considerable time grooming themselves, you shouldn't assume that your cat can groom herself sufficiently well not to require any outside assistance. Whatever type of coat your cat has, you should do some grooming. This will help you keep your cat in tip-top condition and allow you to regularly assess her body for fleas, cuts or lumps, and even weight changes.

Thorough grooming isn't just about aesthetics; it's also essential for the health and comfort of longhair and senior cats who can't maintain their own coats. It's also necessary for a shiny coat and to ensure that enough dead hair is removed from the coat to prevent the kitten from ingesting too much when licking herself, which can lead to problems with fur balls.

A well-kept coat is also better at keeping the kitten warm and dry. An oily lubricating substance called sebum is released by the glands at the base of the hairs, and grooming acts to spread it throughout the coat. When your kitten is exposed to sunlight, this produces vitamin D. Your kitten then ingests this vitamin as she grooms herself. Older, obese, or unwell cats may be unable to groom themselves and so don't benefit from this vitamin.

Cats don't require bathing very often, and most owners do so only if their cat has picked up an unpleasant odor (such as from skunk spray) or if their fur has been contaminated by a dangerous substance, such as oil. Bathing is part of the pre-show preparation for cat show competitors. Set up this chore for success. Cats who are familiar with the bathing process are most comfortable. Bathe your cat in a shallow bowl of warm water, and pour the water over the body rather than placing your cat in a deep bath where she will feel frightened. Towel your cat and allow the coat to dry before brushing through. Use only shampoos that are guaranteed to be suitable for cats since your cat will undoubtedly lick her coat afterward.

Grooming Equipment and Techniques
The types of brushes and combs you need will vary depending upon your kitten's coat type. Most cat owners will need a comb to help untangle the worst knots and to help remove

left: Occasional bathing may be necessary. A shallow basin with a little warm water is ideal.

dead hair. Starting with a wide-tooth comb and then using a finer toothed version will effectively remove dead hair in longer-haired cats. A flea comb can be used to groom the short hair under the chin and on the face.

Never use force while grooming your kitten. Stay relaxed and reward your kitten for allowing you to groom her for a short while. Build up gradually until your kitten allows you to groom for as long as is necessary. Place your kitten on a nonslippery surface or brush her on the floor where she feels most comfortable.

so get into good habits by clipping the tips off each month. This will limit any damage caused while your kitten is playing or climbing on your furniture. Some owners prefer to file the claw tips instead. Before cutting your kitten's nails, refer to our guide in *The Kitten Handbook* on page 27, or ask your veterinarian for a demonstration to avoid any risk of cutting too much of the nail and damaging the sensitive nerve that runs through it.

Nail Care

Kitten claws can be extremely sharp,

Grooming helps create a bond.

Grooming Kit

(General equipment suggested but selection will vary depending on your cat's type of coat)
- Wet wipes to keep eyes and ears clean
- Talcum powder to help with longer coat care
- Combs in a variety of tooth widths
- Slicker brush
- Grooming gloves
- Cat shampoo
- Towel

below: **A range of brushes will keep the coat clean and glossy.**

Soft bristle brush

Comb   *Wire slicker brush*

Recommended Grooming Schedule

Shorthair—once or twice a week

Longhair—daily grooming

Time of year will also influence how much grooming your kitten will require, so be prepared to increase your sessions during the winter.

49

NATURAL CAT BEHAVIOR

If you are able to understand how your kitten is feeling and why she is doing certain things, this insight will help make you a better owner. It will allow you to recognize when your kitten is having fun and when she's feeling frustrated or stressed. Knowing these things will mean that you can then modify your responses accordingly or change things to make your kitten happier. Your kitten will inherit tendencies toward certain behavioral traits, such as vocalization or activity level. If you have researched the breed or know the parents, then you will have a reasonable idea of what to expect. No matter what breed of kitten you have chosen, the behavior patterns can sometimes be confusing or even alarming to a new owner.

Vocalization

Your kitten can make a range of noises to express her feelings. Every cat will have a different voice depending on her breed and experience. Purring occurs in very young kittens to signal their contentment to the queen. Normally, our cat's meows are not a problem, although cats can be encouraged to be overly vocal and those in season will loudly signal their presence by long periods of caterwauling.

Scratching

All cats and kittens need to scratch. This is basic feline behavior. Scratching may seem unnecessary and destructive to us, but it has vital purposes for your kitten. Scratching helps keep their claws healthy and in good condition by causing the older outer sheaths to be shed while exercising the muscles in the legs. Territories are important to cats, and their scratch marking also allows the cat to leave a visual sign of her presence

as well as a scent marker deposited by glands on the feet.

Kneading

You may notice your kitten kneading a blanket or your lap when she's settling down and being petted. The action helps encourage the mother to release milk while a kitten suckles. Many cats will grow out of this behavior. Kittens not weaned properly may knead regularly, and females in heat may also display this behavior more often.

Hunting

Your kitten possesses inherited hunting instincts. While some selective breeding has reduced this desire in many breeds, most cats will still hunt if given the opportunity (even if it is just hunting toys). Kittens begin practicing their hunting skills while with their littermates and will require an outlet for this activity within their new homes. Most are happy pouncing and capturing toys, although some will still instinctively want to hunt small animals and birds outside.

Your Kitten's Body Language

Your kitten will express a lot of her feelings through various body postures. She will use her tail, ears, eyes, and even hair to signal how she feels. Although these signals can be very complex, the postures (shown right) can be a good indicator of mood.

A Kitten's Body Language

Happy and Relaxed Kitten	Ears are upright, whiskers sit out from face; tail is relaxed and curled around body during relaxation or held erect as she approaches
Anxious Kitten	Ears are twisted and leaning backward; the tail will be low or held close to the body
Frightened Kitten	Ears are flattened back on head, the whiskers are also pulled back against the face, and the tail may be puffed up and lowered; the back may be arched
Irritated Kitten	Tip of the tail starts to flick and flicking will increase in vigour as irritation increases; ears may begin to turn away from you
Defensive Kitten	The back is often arched, the tail is puffed up and arched; ears are flattened to the side

left: Relaxation is indicated by soft eyes, upright ears, and neutral whiskers.

Back arched

Whiskers pulled back

right: A defensive kitten will puff her tail and may twist her ears.

left: Fear signals are well defined. The kitten makes herself small and flattens the ears and whiskers. She will prepare to escape if possible.

SOCIALIZATION

Socialization is the process whereby a kitten learns to familiarize herself with and feel confident during interactions with people, pets, and other elements of her environment. We know that a kitten experiences a sensitive period between two and eight weeks when she's especially able to learn to feel happy about new events.

Enjoying lots of pleasant experiences during this time is essential in order for the kitten to grow up to be a confident and friendly cat. This is why it's so important to choose breeders who allow their kittens to be handled between 30 minutes and 1 hour per day. Kittens who have not been handled, such as those living in barns or springing from feral litters, are less likely to grow up to feel relaxed around people.

Socializing Up to 13 Weeks

Gentle, pleasant handling teaches the kitten to tolerate petting, grooming, and health care in the future.

left: **Kittens need to experience household equipment and noises.**

Socializing after your kitten comes home—You should begin gently introducing your kitten to new people, other pets, and noise-making household equipment, such as vacuum cleaners and washing machines. Leave the cat carrier out so your kitten remains comfortable going into it and when traveling in there. Your kitten should experience some short trips in the car that don't always end up in the vet's or a boarding kennel so that she doesn't learn to associate only stressful times with traveling. Remember that your kitten should meet people of different ages, including children if you think that she may live with some in the future. Noises can startle a kitten, so it can be a great idea to use a sound effects CD to gently introduce noises to which it may be hard to arrange exposure otherwise. These CDs are widely available and are often used for puppy socialization as well.

Continue socializing your kitten through introduction to different people and new events throughout the first year of her life.

Training Your Kitten

Although kittens are not traditionally trained in the way that dogs are, your kitten will be influenced by your responses to her behavior. Kittens are intelligent animals and will learn from their experiences. They may not have the same attention span for training as a dog has, but they will work for a reward, which means that you can shape their behavior. With patience and consistency, you can encourage a range of desirable actions.

Rewards—A reward is anything that your cat loves. Usually we use edible treats, but a cat will also enjoy a game with a favorite toy. Cats become bored very quickly when offered the same treat over and over again, so keep the treats small and vary what you offer. You'll soon discover what works best for your kitten. Remember to keep training sessions very short for maximum effect.

Toys will encourage your kitten to approach.

right: **With socialization, your kitten will be confident around people.**

kitten and rewarding her for responding. Soon, your kitten will learn to rush to you for attention or treats when you call.

Punishment—Cats do not respond well to being punished, so never smack your kitten if she makes a mistake. Instead distract

above: **Call your kitten's name and encourage her to approach you. Then make sure you reward her with a treat you know she loves.**

your kitten and then encourage a more appropriate behavior. If your kitten consistently responds incorrectly, consider why she doesn't understand or what may be preventing her from performing the action to your satisfaction.

below right: **Some cats will prefer a toy rather than an edible titbit as a reward.**

Timing—Getting the timing of your rewards right is very important, or your kitten will become confused and your training may take longer. When you're training make sure that your treat jar is close by and that you praise and pet as soon as your kitten gets it right.

Early lessons—The first lesson you can teach your kitten is to come when you call her name. This will then allow you to call your kitten inside more easily. Many owners begin to teach this skill without consciously realizing they are training their kitten. In order to make this response more reliable, you should spend some time each day calling your

Cats are attracted to toys that they can chase and pounce on.

NEUTERING AND SPAYING

Neutering is the removal of the cat's reproductive organs. The action of neutering a male cat is called castration, while neutering a female is called spaying. Responsible owners of pet cats who do not want to breed from them usually choose to neuter since there are so many homeless and unwanted cats and kittens in the world anyway. There is no point in risking further unplanned pregnancies and unwanted offspring.

Unless you have purchased your kitten with the intention of becoming a breeder and taking on all the major responsibilities and financial costs that this will incur, you should have your kitten neutered. Your veterinarian will advise you as to when this should be done. Since kittens mature sexually very early, it's important that they are neutered before any accidental matings can occur. The operations are often carried out at approximately five to six months of age and involve a quick, routine operation under general anesthetic.

The Female Cycle

A female cat will come into her heat cycle, or estrus, at certain times of year when the day length is correct. Most kittens are born in the spring and summer months. When a female comes into season, she will exhibit certain behavioral changes including vocalizing and spraying. Unless she is mated, she will come into season again three weeks later. This will continue throughout the breeding season. During this time you will notice the female becoming very friendly, rolling on the floor and taking up the mating posture.

Castrating a Male Cat

This operation involves the removal of both testicles through a very small incision that normally heals without the need for any stitches.

Spaying a Female Cat

This operation involves a flank (*above*) or midline incision through which the ovaries and the uterus are removed. The wound is then stitched together. Your cat will receive appropriate pain relief medication and will recover surprisingly quickly within a few days. Some cats have to wear a plastic collar to prevent them from licking their wounds. The hair will grow back and there will be very little if any outward sign of the operation. You may have

above: **A male kitten has visible testicles below his tail. These are removed during castration.**

> **Expert Tip**
> Kittens can mature at a surprisingly young age, especially in the case of some of the more exotic breeds, so be aware of this and separate sexes or neuter early to avoid unwanted pregnancies.

to return to your surgeon to have the stitches removed after approximately 10 days. Other types of stitches dissolve over time.

Despite popular belief, spayed and neutered cats are not more prone to becoming inactive and gaining weight than intact felines. After the operation, maintain daily playtime with your cat and pay attention to the amount of food you feed her to keep her at a healthy weight and enjoy a happy temperament.

Remember to consider any agreement that you have signed with the breeder. You may have signed a contract to ensure that you never breed from your kitten, in which case neutering would be advisable. If you have agreed to show or breed your kitten, then you'll have to refrain from neutering until you have fulfilled your commitments.

below: **An Elizabethan collar will prevent your cat from licking her wounds.**

below: **A female in season will mate frequently, and kittens within a litter may have different sires.**

Kittens quickly recover after neutering.

Benefits of Castrating a Tom

- No unwanted kittens
- Urine spraying within the home is reduced
- Roaming behavior lessens so less likely to get lost or be involved in a road traffic accident
- Less likely to fight other males, which reduces the likelihood of injury and disease transmission
- Less pungent urine

Benefits of Spaying a Queen

- No unwanted kittens
- Does not attract roaming tomcats
- Removes spraying during her heat cycle
- No risk of pyometra (infection of the uterus)
- No "calling" when in season
- Will not try to escape from the home to seek a mate

ACCIDENTS AND FIRST AID

Being prepared is the best first step to dealing with an injury problem. Assemble a first aid kit complete with appropriate medical equipment and emergency contact numbers so that you can act as calmly and efficiently as possible should the need arise to use it after an accident.

> **Safety Tip**
> ● Ensure that you have a fully equipped first aid kit to hand at home (see page 19 for details), and keep a note of your vet's number by your telephone.

Bleeding

Cuts and grazes—Gently bathe small wounds with a saline solution (use about half a teaspoonful of salt diluted in a large tub of warm water) and apply a dressing to protect the wound from infection. If you're in any doubt, please ask your vet to check it, as infections can be serious.

Internal bleeding—If you notice unexplained blood coming from your cat's nose, mouth, or anus, then seek veterinary help. Calmly and carefully transport the kitten in her carrier to your vet for urgent help. A less obvious symptom of internal bleeding is pale gums and cold limbs.

External bleeding—Certain parts of your cat will bleed more profusely than others, so stay calm and assess what you're dealing with. Ear nicks can appear like serious wounds until they are cleaned up. However a large wound, or one that continues to bleed, will need attention. If your cat

is bleeding badly; then you should gently put pressure on the area with a dressing and bandage. Serious bleeds may require a tourniquet to limit blood loss while you get to your vet's surgery. In such cases, apply a flat tape to an area between the bleed and the heart, then twist it to stem the blood flow, but time when you started to make sure you don't keep it tight for more than 15 minutes. This is a strictly short-term procedure while on your way to obtain professional help.

Stings

When removing a bee sting, be careful not to squeeze more poison into your cat by scraping it out rather than pinching with tweezers. Soothe the pain by bathing the area in either diluted vinegar solution (for wasp stings) or bicarbonate of soda solution (for bee stings). If you notice any excessive swelling or if your cat is having trouble breathing after a sting, seek help from your vet.

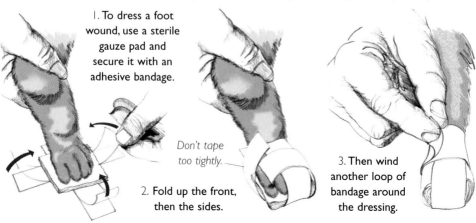

1. To dress a foot wound, use a sterile gauze pad and secure it with an adhesive bandage.

Don't tape too tightly.

2. Fold up the front, then the sides.

3. Then wind another loop of bandage around the dressing.

Cat Bites

All cat bites should be considered serious, as they often become infected and may form an abscess if left untreated. Bite wounds often appear small and nonproblematic, but actually the puncture wound will often carry many bacteria from the aggressor cat's mouth. Carefully cut away surrounding fur and bathe twice daily with a saline solution. Larger injuries or weeping wounds should be assessed by your vet, who will decide whether to prescribe antibiotics.

above: **Some wounds require a dressing that limits movement. Keep your kitten indoors and make sure she can climb into the litter box.**

Road Traffic Accident (RTA)

Stay safe and make sure you don't put yourself in danger on the road. Carefully lift the kitten and place her in your cat carrier so movement is restricted and so she isn't further stressed on the way to the vet. Keep the carrier dark and quiet. Call your vet's office to advise them that you're on your way and so they can give you advice.

below: **Don't delay taking an injured cat to the vet for expert assessment.**

Burns

As is true when treating humans, the quicker you respond to a burn, the less damage will be sustained. Cool the area with water or an ice pack and take your kitten to the vet. Don't put on any ointments or bandages, and prevent your cat from licking or scratching the injury.

Poison

If you suspect that your kitten has ingested a toxic substance, then you should seek urgent veterinary attention. Never try to induce vomiting, as this can be very dangerous. Try to prevent your cat from licking any noxious substance from her coat. Post the phone number of your closest emergency veterinary clinic on your refrigerator door.

Snake Bite

A cat may come into contact with a snake that slithers inside the home or in an outdoor enclosure. If possible, identify the snake, but do not endanger yourself. Seek immediate veterinary help, and keep your cat's movements to a minimum by placing her in a cat carrier.

TRAVEL ARRANGEMENTS

When you take on ownership of a cat, you must create a plan that addresses holidays, work travel, or emergency situations. All owners should make plans for their cats to be cared for while they're away. This includes overnight stays and longer trips. You should never leave your cat alone while you are on vacation. There should always be someone present who is responsible for the daily care of your cat.

> **Expert Tip**
> Senior cats may find it harder to cope with change. If you board your cat, realize that she may require extra blankets to feel calm and cozy.

idea for the caregiver to know what symptoms to look out for and how to respond if they occur. Leave written consent to allow this person to make medical decisions while you're away.

There are a few options to choose from, depending upon how long you will be going away, your cat's temperament, and obviously the cost. See the chart opposite for a range of choices.

You must leave clear instructions about your cat's requirements with the person who will provide care. If your cat is prone to any health problems, such as urinary tract infections, it is a good

Checklist for Leaving Your Kitten with a Caregiver

- Leave a diet plan stating preferences, amounts to feed, and your cat's routine.
- List any medications your cat is on, and state clearly when they should be given.
- Leave the name, address, and telephone number of your cat's vet.
- Set out the grooming equipment so that your cat's coat isn't neglected.
- Provide your cell phone and email address to this person.
- Place your cat carrier out so that the person has it readily to hand in case of emergencies.

Checklist for Leaving Your Kitten in a Boarding Facility

- Leave a diet plan stating preferences, amounts to feed, and normal feeding routine.
- List any medications your cat is on, and state clearly when they should be given.
- Supply vaccination records.
- Leave health records if your cat has a problem that may need attention during its stay.
- Leave the vet's name, address, and telephone number.
- Supply familiar bedding to ease transition and help with settling in.
- Leave out some favorite toys.

> **Expert Tip**
> Keep your cat's parasite prevention care up to date to maximize protection and prevent cross-infection while she is in the cattery.

Who Will Look After My Kitten?

Friend or Family Member 	If you have reliable family members or friends, they may agree to provide care and company for your cat while you're away. For some cats, this is less unsettling than being taken away from their familiar surroundings. It is also a cheaper option. The person you choose can get to know your cat and her routine before your vacation by frequently making visits to your home.
Professional Pet Sitter	A professional pet sitter may be able to commit more time to caring for your cat. This is especially true if you have several cats or if they need specialized grooming or care. Choose only an insured and recommended professional who can prove they're trustworthy. Always check references. Ideally ask a trusted friend or neighbor for a recommendation, or ask advice from your vet clinic staff.
Boarding Facility	If your cat is upset by encountering new people in your home or if leaving your home in the care of a stranger is unappealing, a boarding facility may be ideal. They vary from very basic cat cages to luxurious suites with TV sets. Ask for recommendations and visit the facility before booking a reservation.. You will need to provide evidence that your cat is up to date on her vaccinations. Be aware there may be added fees for administering necessary medicaitons to your cat.
Vet Boarding	If your cat has ongoing medical problems and you're going away for just a few days, then you may choose to board her at your veterinary clinic This is less suitable for extended vacations since most vet surgeries have only limited space and often don't have access to an indoor space in which the cat can exercise safely.

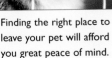

Finding the right place to leave your pet will afford you great peace of mind.

INDEX

PICTURE CREDITS

Bayer HealthCare: 46 left.
Bigstockphoto.com:
Jaimie Duplass: 43 center right.
Jane Burton, Warren Photographic: Back cover top left, back cover bottom right, cover front flap, 1, 2, 3, 6 bottom, 7 top left, 10 bottom left, 14 bottom left, 15 bottom, 18 top, 19 bottom left, 20 left, 20-21, 21 center right, 24 bottom, 25 top, 26, 26-27, 27 top right, 27 center right, 28 center, 29 all three images, 30 bottom, 31 top, 43 center left, 43 bottom left, 44 bottom left, 45 top right, 47 bottom right, 51 bottom left, 51 bottom right, 52-53, 53 bottom right, 54 bottom left, 55 top right, 55 center right, 57 top right, 57 bottom left, 58 top left.
Crestock.com:
Norman Chan: 37 (kibble).
Dreamstime.com:
Hanhanpeggy: 59 bottom left. Patrick Hermans: 22 (food bowl). Kalvis Kalsers: 11 left. Stuart Key: 17 top left. Caroline Klapper: 33 top right. Michael Pettigrew: 48 bottom left. Kristian Sekulic: Cover back flap, 11 bottom right. Anna Utekhina: 50 top left. Oscar Williams: 17 top center. Lu Zhang: 59 bottom right.
Fotolia.com:
Tony Campbell: 21 top center, 21 bottom right. Katerina Cherkashina: 7 bottom left. Willee Cole: 34 left, 35 bottom right. Evgenij Gorbunov: 50 bottom left. Eric Isselée: 7 center right, 15 top right. Natalia Lisovskaya: 17 top right, 21 top right, 33 center, 33 bottom right. Monika 3 Steps Ahead: 40 bottom left. Antonio Nunes: 8 bottom. Nikolay Okhitin: 9 center right. Andrejs Pidjass: 39 top right. Kristian Sekulic: 11 bottom right, 12 center left. Ferenc Szelepesenyi: 36 bottom. Mykola Velychko: 25 bottom.
Interpet Archive: Back cover center, 16 both, 17 bottom right, 18 bottom, 19 bottom right, 30 top left, 32 center, 37 (canned and moist food), 48 top center, 49 bottom left and right, 54 top right.

iStockphoto.com:
Ira Bachinskaya: 44 bottom center. Hagit Berkovich: 55 center left. Grigory Bibikov: 5 top left. Mariya Bibikova: Front cover (main image). Tony Campbell: 12 center, 34 top right. Katerina Cherkashina: 50 top right. Lars Christensen: 32 bottom left. Christina Claus: 19 bottom center. Rhienna Cutler: 13 bottom, 45 bottom. Joe Gough: 31 bottom left. Mark Hayes: 23 left. JoeLena: 41 center, 41 right. Joe_Potato: 33 bottom left. Zsolt Langviser: 19 top right. Lcocci 42 bottom left. Sandra Nicol: 36 top left. Skip O'Donnell: 27 top left. Przemyslaw Rzeszutko: 24 center. Mehmet Salih: 5 center right. Kristian Sekulic: Back cover top right, 22 top right. Vika Valter: 53 top right. Walik: 52 center left.
Merial Animal Health Ltd: 46 (louse and mite micrographs).
Shutterstock Inc.:
Tony Campbell: 9 bottom right, 14 center right, 22 left, 28 top, 42 top, 43 top, 55 center, 59 top left, 59 center left. Lars Christensen: 33 center right. Elnur: 12 top. Jeanne Hatch: 4. Frenck and Danielle Kaufmann: 49 top. Vladimir Mihajlovich Suponev: 6 top. Ariusz Nawrocki: 39 bottom left, 51 center left. Perrush: 37 bottom, 40-41. Sergey Petrov: 31 bottom right. Robynrg: 38 top left, 40 top right. Ferenc Szelepesenyi: Cover (front inset), 5 top right, 35 top right. Nikolay Titov: 8 top left, 10 top, 38 bottom, 45 top center, 52 top center. Miroslav Tolimir: 36 top right. H Tuller 58 bottom left. Anna Utekhina: 24 top, 47 top. Darja Vorontsova: 23 bottom right.
Hardback case: Interpet Publishing Archive (front cover center right), Dreamstime.com/ Tony Campbell (back cover top right), iStock.com/Tony Campbell (front cover center left), iStock.com/Tony Campbell/Rafal Zdeb (front cover top montage), Shutterstock.com/ Tony Campbell (spine), Warren Photographic (back cover top left and bottom, inside endpaper).